curiousabout

SLOTHS

BY AMY S. HANSEN

AMICUS • AMICUS INK

What are you

curious about?

CHAPTER THREE

3

Sloth Families
PAGE
18

Curious About is published
by Amicus and Amicus Ink
P.O. Box 227
Mankato, MN 56002
www.amicuspublishing.us

Designer: Aubrey Harper
Photo researcher: Bridget Prehn
Editor: Alissa Thielges
Series Designer: Kathleen Petelinsek

Library of Congress Cataloging-in-Publication Data
Names: Hansen, Amy, author. Title: Curious about sloths
/ by Amy S. Hansen. Description: Mankato, MN :
Amicus, [2023] | Series: Curious about wild animals |
Includes bibliographical references and index. |
Audience: Ages 6–9 | Audience: Grades 2–3
Identifiers: LCCN 2020000578 (print) | LCCN
2020000579 (ebook) | ISBN 9781645491378
(library binding) | ISBN 9781681527048 (paper-
back) | ISBN 9781645491798 (pdf) Subjects: LCSH:
Sloths—Juvenile literature. Classification: LCC QL737.
E2 H19 2023 (print) | LCC QL737.E2 (ebook) | DDC
599.3/13—dc23 LC record available at
https://lccn.loc.gov/2020000578
LC ebook record available at
https://lccn.loc.gov/2020000579

Photos © Shutterstock/Inspired By Maps cover, 1;
Shutterstock/kungverylucky 2 (left), 5; Minden/Suzi
Eszterhas 2 (right), 14–15; Minden/Christian Ziegler
3, 20–21; Alamy/Rosanne Tackaberry 6; Dreamstime/
Brooke Parish 7; Pixabay/SpencerWing 8 (flowers);
iStock/Vichailao 8 (twigs); Flickr/Gary Yankech 8
(bugs); iStock/ca2hill 8 (fruit); Shutterstock/Deplanque
Joel 8 (leaves); iStock/Freder 9; Minden/Suzi Eszterhas
10-11; Alamy/Harry Collins 12; iStock/naturediver 13
(slug); iStock/filipfoto 13 (snail); iStock/malerapaso 13
(starfish); iStock/GlobalP 13 (sloth); Shutterstock/Smileus
13 (giant tortoise); iStock/KenCanning 16–17; Minden/
Suzi Eszterhas 19; Shutterstock/Dn Br 22 and (sloth);
Freepik.com 22 and 23 (palm tree)

CHAPTER ONE

Where do sloths live?

In trees! They live in **rain forests** in Central and South America. They hang on tree branches. Long claws help them hold on. Sloths spend 90 percent of their life hanging upside down.

North America

Central America

■ Sloth range

South America

Sloth bodies have adapted to life upside down.

Is there more than one kind of sloth?

Two-toed sloth

Yes. There are two kinds. Two-toed sloths have two front claws. Three-toed sloths have three front claws. Giant sloths lived thousands of years ago. They are now **extinct**. They were as big as elephants!

Three-toed sloth

DID YOU KNOW?
Sloths are the slowest mammals on Earth. They move about 7 feet (2.1 m) in a minute.

What do sloths eat?

Leaves. But a sloth will eat whatever it can reach. They eat buds and berries, too. Plants do not give sloths much energy. The food can take weeks to **digest**. This is one of the reasons they are slow.

Flowers

Leaves

DID YOU KNOW?
Sloths are omnivores.
They eat plants
and insects.

Twigs

Bugs

Fruit

Leaves don't have a lot of nutrients for sloths.

What dangers do sloths face?

Crossing roads is dangerous for slow-moving sloths.

Sloths are hunted by other animals. But the main danger is humans. They cut down trees. Sloths do not know where to go. Some countries have set up **reserves**. The land is protected there. A sloth's home is safe.

What do sloths do?

Sloths' limbs lock when they sleep. They don't fall.

Sleep and eat. Sloths sleep 15 hours a day. When they wake up, they eat. They move only if they have to. Then they rest. This changes at **mating** time. A female will call out "ahh-eeee!" Male sloths wake up. They go find her.

BANANA
SLUG

6.5 INCHES (16.5 CM)
PER MINUTE

SNAIL

2.6 FEET (0.8 M)
PER MINUTE

SEA STAR

3.3 FEET (1 M)
PER MINUTE

SLOTH

7 FEET (2.1 M)
PER MINUTE

GIANT
TORTOISE

14.1 FEET (4.2 M)
PER MINUTE

Are sloths lazy?

No. They are hiding. Hawks and jaguars eat sloths. They watch for quick movements. Sloths move slowly. They stay safe. It is hard for sloths to walk on land. Their legs can't support them. Their claws get in the way, too. But they are good swimmers.

Sloths move easily in water.

DID YOU KNOW?

When the rain forest floods, a sloth may swim to a new tree.

Why are some sloths green?

The type of algae on sloths' fur doesn't grow anywhere else.

That's **algae**. It grows on calm, wet surfaces. Sloths' fur is always wet. Sloths do not move much. Their fur is the perfect place for algae to grow. The green fur is good for sloths. It helps them blend in with the trees.

What are baby sloths like?

Babies are clingy. They hold onto their mother as she moves. They drink her milk. They eat small bites of her food. After six months, a baby sloth can live on its own. It doesn't move far. Sloth families stay close for years. Young sloths have a lot to learn.

A mother sloth teaches her baby what to eat.

Young sloths hang on to mom until they are strong enough to hang by themselves.

Do baby sloths ever fall?

DID YOU KNOW?
Sloths are incredibly strong. They have 52 different arm muscles. A human has 23.

Sometimes. Even grown sloths can fall. But sloths are sturdy. They don't usually get hurt from a fall. Mothers teach babies how to hold on. They show babies how to use their claws. Babies practice a lot. They build strong muscles.

ASK MORE QUESTIONS

How can sloths hang upside down without getting tired?

Where are the sloth reserves located?

Try a BIG QUESTION: How are sloths important to the rain forest?

SEARCH FOR ANSWERS

Search the library catalog or the Internet.
A librarian, teacher, or parent can help you.

Using Keywords
Find the looking glass.

Keywords are the most important words in your question.

If you want to know about:

- how sloths can live upside down, type: SLOTH ANATOMY

- protecting sloths, type: SLOTH CONSERVATION

FIND GOOD SOURCES

Here are some good, safe sources you can use in your research.

Your librarian can help you find more.

Books

How Sloths Grow Up
by Linda Bozzo, 2020.

Sloths by Marysa Storm, 2020.

Internet Sites

Nat Geo Kids | Sloths
*https://kids.nationalgeographic.com/
animals/mammals/sloth*
National Geographic is a respected news organization. It reports on nature and animals.

San Diego Zoo Kids | Two-Toed Sloth
*https://kids.sandiegozoo.org/
animals/two-toed-sloth*
The San Diego Zoo is a respected U.S. zoo. It funds research to help save animals.

Every effort has been made to ensure that these websites are appropriate for children. However, because of the nature of the Internet, it is impossible to guarantee that these sites will remain active indefinitely or that their contents will not be altered.

SHARE AND TAKE ACTION

Visit a local zoo.
Talk with a zookeeper about sloths.

Move like a sloth.
Do something in slow motion. Or try hanging upside down. What muscles do you use?

Raise money for sloths.
Help protect them and the rain forest.

GLOSSARY

algae A plant-like organism that lives in wet, still places, often found in ponds.

digest To break down food to make energy for the body.

extinct No longer found living in the world; known only from fossils.

mammal A type of animal that breathes air with lungs and feeds milk to its young.

mating When a male and female come together to make a baby.

rain forest A forest ecosystem that is constantly wet because of rain.

reserve A place where land is set aside and protected so plants and animals are safe.

INDEX

About the Author

Amy S. Hansen lives with her husband, two sons, and a dog in Maryland. She has also lived in Wisconsin, Ohio, and Michigan. One of her favorite parts of her job is doing research and finding out fun facts. Those facts made these books very fun to write.